What CAN I Be?

By Robert Little

Illustrated by Audrey Fitzpatrick

RELDE Publishing

Little, Robert, 1959-
    What can I be? / by Robert Little; illustrated by
Audrey Fitzpatrick. -- 1st ed.
    p. cm.
    SUMMARY: Jamaal, an eleven-year-old African American
boy confused about what he can become, seeks advice from
an elderly gentleman, Mr. Cleo.
    Audience: Ages 9-11.
    ISBN 0-970-18633-9

    1. Self-esteem--Juvenile fiction. 2. Self-esteem--
Fiction. I. Fitzpatrick, Audrey. II. Title.

    PZ7.L7253Wha 2001   (E)
        QB101-700905

For additional books and to contact Robert Little
for speaking engagements:
RELDE Publishing, LLC
P.O. Box 21304, Jackson, MS 39289
(601) 968-9052
www.reldepublishing.com
www.robertlittlespeaker.com

DEDICATION

This book is dedicated to the two most influential males
in my life, my father, Willie Little, whose likeness is
represented by Mr. Cleo and my son, Elliott Little,
whose likeness is represented by Jamaal. Additionally,
I dedicate this book to all young men that I have been
privileged to mentor.
        — R. L.

This book is dedicated to my son, Christopher, my
father, Charles, and my husband, Prentiss who support
me in my endeavors to use my talents to help others.
Their patience and understanding have enabled me to
use my gifts to benefit others. My prayer is that this
book is well received into the lives of all who read its
pages.
        — A. F.

As Mr. Cleo walked down the hallway toward the gymnasium, he looked out of a doorway window and noticed Jamaal leaning up against a wall looking sad. Mr. Cleo, a custodian at Maples Middle School, always tried to help Jamaal, an 11-year-old fifth grader.

Whenever Mr.Cleo saw Jamaal, he always reminded him to pull his *pants* up, keep his *grades* up, and hold his *head* up. Even though there were plenty of other students that could've used the same advice, Mr. Cleo always felt the need to share it with Jamaal.

Jamaal was a rather small kid for his age. He never spoke very much, but he spent a lot of time wondering about things. He was the oldest of his sister and two brothers. He always looked as if all the pressures of the world were on his shoulders. Jamaal rarely ever smiled. In some ways, Jamaal reminded Mr. Cleo of himself when he was 11-years-old.

Jamaal made average grades most of the time and actually liked social studies. He had an interest in basketball, but was far from a superstar. As a matter of fact, he was often one of the last ones chosen when playing a pick-up game in the neighborhood. That didn't bother him too much, though.

"What's wrong Jamaal, did somebody take your belt?" jokingly asked Mr. Cleo. He knew Jamaal usually didn't wear a belt. He would always tell Mr. Cleo that he forgot it, knowing all the time he wanted his pants to sag.

"No sir," replied Jamaal as he glanced up at Mr. Cleo.

"Well, is something ailin' ya?" Mr. Cleo wanted to know.

"No sir," Jamaal commented, always very respectful to Mr. Cleo.

"Well, what's the problem, then?" Mr. Cleo said in a concerned voice.

"Oh, nothing," expressed Jamaal with a very low voice.

"Young man, I wasn't born yesterday. What's the matter?" exclaimed Mr. Cleo.

t first thought, Jamaal didn't care to discuss it, but he knew Mr. Cleo was really concerned. Then, he realized that maybe Mr. Cleo could help. So he said, "I guess I'm confused. We were talking about what we wanted to be when we grow up in my 4th period class today and I just —I just don't know."

"What do you want to be when you grow up?" asked Mr. Cleo, fully expecting Jamaal to say a doctor, scientist, lawyer or schoolteacher.

"Well, I don't know," replied Jamaal, while looking down at the sidewalk. "That's the problem—I really don't know, Mr. Cleo."

"Do you like working with your hands? Do you like science? Do you like helping people?" asked Mr. Cleo, firing one question after another. He was determined to get some kind of answer from Jamaal, or at least to get him thinking about it.

"No, Mr. Cleo, you don't understand," Jamaal expressed, while shaking his head.

"Well, that's OK," said Mr. Cleo, while putting his hand on Jamaal's shoulder. "Most boys your age really don't know what they want to be when they grow up. You'll decide soon enough. I bet you will."

Jamaal suddenly looked up at Mr. Cleo with teary eyes and a confused look on his face. "Mr. Cleo, I don't know what I can be. WHAT CAN I BE?" he mumbled while trying to fight back tears.

Mr. Cleo realized this wasn't something to be taken lightly. Jamaal was very upset while thinking about what he could be in life.

"Come over here and sit down with me lil' fellow," said Mr. Cleo as they both took a seat on the steps.

"Young man, listen to me and listen to me good. You can be anything you want to be, if you put your mind to it. Do you hear me?" said Mr. Cleo as he looked up toward the heavens.

Right away, lots of reasons to fail came to Jamaal's mind.

"...But, I live in a poor neighborhood."

"That's OK. I do, too, and so did all six of my children," replied Mr. Cleo. "They went on to make something of themselves and I know you can, too. I know there are times at night when you can hear gun shots and you want to get under the bed, thinking the next bullet might come through the window. I know there are times when you leave home hoping that somebody won't break in and steal what you have. I know there are vacant houses—some being used for illegal things, some falling in, but that's OK. I know these things, Jamaal. I see them, too.

"Where you're from can make you bitter or it can make you better. It's your choice. But if you choose to have this to make you better, then these are the things that'll drive you to try to do something with your life. But, Jamaal, you gotta remember this—It ain't where you from—
what matters is where you're going."

"...But, they call me 'at-risk'."

"That's OK. You need to learn early in life that people will always call you something. But, just because a person calls you something doesn't mean you have to be it. Let me give you an example. You're a millionaire. I just called you a millionaire, Jamaal. Are you a millionaire?"

"Mr. Cleo, you know I'm not a millionaire," Jamaal answered with a smirk on his face.

"I know you ain't a millionaire, and I also know you have what it takes to be what you wanna be, too. Do you get my point?" asked Mr. Cleo. "You see, Jamaal to you, 'at-risk' should mean 'at-risk' to be successful in life. For those people that call you 'at-risk,' give them an early invitation to your college graduation."

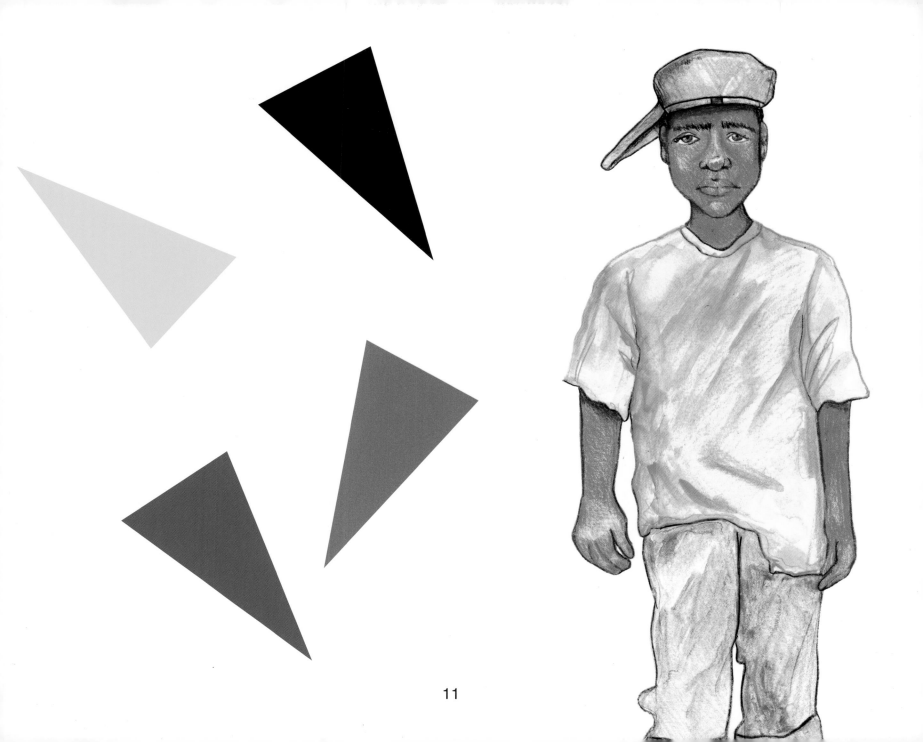

"...But, I hardly ever see my daddy."

"These days, many daddies ain't living with their families. But, that's why it's important for you to help your momma with things around the house. She could use the help, I'm sure. Learn how to take care of your sister and little brothers, take out the trash, sweep the floors, wash the dishes and clothes, mow the lawn and cook. As you learn to do these things, you'll be learning responsibility. That way, you'll be better able to do things for your own family someday.

"You also need to remember how it feels not having your daddy around. I know when you see other children with their daddies, you wish that you could be with yours. I know there are things that you just don't want to talk about with your momma, and you wish your daddy was around. Well, you need to remember these times and how they feel to you, so that your children will never have to feel that way."

"...But my friends will call me names if I'm smarter than they are."

"They will call you names?" asked Mr. Cleo.

"Yes sir," replied Jamaal. "They will call me names like nerd and geek."

"Remember what I told you a few minutes ago, people will always call you something. They also have names that they call people who don't do their work in school too, don't they? And, those names are a lot worse than nerd and geek. But, if your friends call you names for getting good grades Jamaal, you might be hanging out with the wrong group.

"The people you need to be spending time with are the ones that understand how important it is to make 90's and 100's on tests. Trying to do your best shows you are a hard worker and you know what you want out of life. No, don't let name-calling stop you from doing your best."

 ut, I don't wear 'tight' clothes."

"Son, why do you want to wear your clothes tight?" asked Mr. Cleo.

"Huh, Mr. Cleo," said Jamaal. "I don't mean tight, tight. I mean designer clothes."

"Jamaal, it's more important to go to school clean than it is to wear 'tight' clothes. You should never feel that who you are is decided by the clothes you wear. Your smarts and what's in your heart are what really matter. They make you the person that you are. The stuff that's on the inside is what counts. But Jamaal, instead of worrying about 'tight' clothes that you don't have, think about becoming the person who designs those clothes. That way, people will walk around wearing your name, instead of you walking around advertising their clothes. Think about being the person who owns the store that sells those clothes. One thing you gotta remember is you gotta think more about owning things, instead of buying things.

"Shucks boy, I can remember when I was your age, I had to wear the same clothes three days a week—talking about 'tight' clothes, hah. I can remember my younger brothers wearing my clothes when they got too little for me. Momma would patch' em up and we would wear those clothes for years."

"Ah, c'mon Mr. Cleo," remarked Jamaal.

"Ain't foolin' ya, son. You don't know how blessed you are."

"...But, people say things will never change for Black people."

"They say this because they're not trying to change things themselves. Sure enough, there are people in this world that don't want things to be any better for Blacks, but most people don't feel that way. Yes, we Black people are sometimes not treated fairly, but you can't let that stop you.

"People that think the right way will do good in life. The way to think is—if I can do better, then things as they are, ain't good enough. In order to bring about change in the world, you must start with yourself. I was always taught to treat everybody the way I wanted to be treated. Most people try to do that. I wish everybody did.

"And for those people that say, 'Things will never change for Black people,' I just have to say, thank goodness, things ain't like they used to be."

B
ut, I don't do math as good as Andre."

"There are different kinds of smarts," said Mr. Cleo. "Just because you don't do math as good as someone else, don't mean you ain't smart. I'm sure you're good in other subjects, music, sports or other things. If you ain't, it's because you ain't trying.

"For too long, people have been told that just because a person don't do good in math or science, they ain't smart. That causes a lot of people to believe that they can't do good in life. That's the biggest fib I've ever heard.

Now, Jamaal, don't get me wrong, it's very important to do your best in every subject. You should always give it your best—I don't care what it is. When you do good in all of your subjects it makes you a better person, which will be good for you in whatever you do. But, just because you don't do good in one subject don't mean you ain't smart and you won't do good in life."

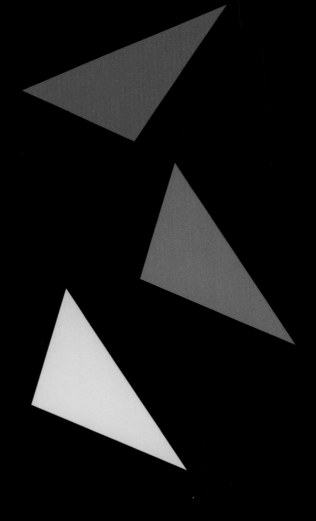

"...But, I don't play basketball like *'Smooth'.*"

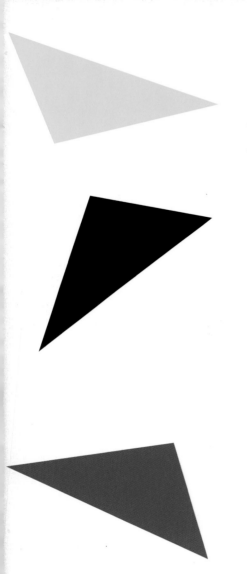

"Even though basketball may be *Smooth's* talent, we all have our own talents. God gave us all different talents and gifts. Can you imagine what the world would be like if we all had the same talents? Never compare your talents to others. There will always be people that can do some things better than you. That's the way life is. But, you must remember, you can always do something better than most other people. That could be your talent. What you have to do is find out what it is that you do better than most people and learn to do it better and better and better.

"This means things other than sports, too. Too many young, Black males are planning on becoming famous ball players. Most don't make it. Chances of becoming a doctor are much greater than the chances of becoming a famous basketball player."

"...But, people are always telling me what I can't do."

"In life, there are going to always be people that will tell you what you can't do. They all have their own reasons for doing this. Some of these people might be your friends. They may see your talents and skills, but because they don't have them, they want to stop you from using yours. Others may be older people that truly care about you, but they have tried to do big things in life themselves and failed. They don't want you to become hurt and disappointed like them. Don't listen to people that tell you what you can't do. If you truly want to do something, you can. Just believe that you can and go do it.

"By the way, you don't ever have to argue with anybody about what you can do in life. Don't even waste your time. You have more important things to be doing. Just leave those people alone and get on with your business."

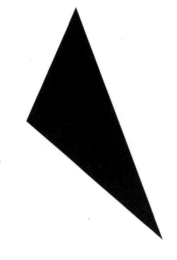

"...But, there are gangs on my street."

"Most people who join gangs join because they want to belong to something. Many times, it's because they don't feel loved by their family. Some join because they have too much time on their hands and are not putting it to good use.

"Stay clear of gangs, Jamaal. If you want to belong to a gang to feel respected, honored or loved, try the gangs at your school—basketball team, football team or the honor roll gang."

"...But, what if I'm not Black enough?"

"What if you're not Black enough? Now, Jamaal, you've gotta explain that one to me," said Mr. Cleo.

"Well, Mr. Cleo, if you talk right," explained Jamaal, "you know, use proper grammar, there are some people who will say you are trying to talk proper or they'll say you're trying to be White. There are even people that say golf, soccer or tennis is not a Black man's game. That's what I mean about not being Black enough.

"Jamaal there were times when we spoke only what we knew how to speak and maybe it wasn't good English, but we did the best we could. Now, you know better and you should do better.

"As far as sports is concerned, go out and play whatever you like. Who cares whether it's a Black man's game or a White man's game. If you play it well enough and can get paid millions of dollars to play it—it becomes Jamaal's game. Go tell Tiger Woods that golf is a White man's game, hah."

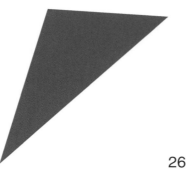

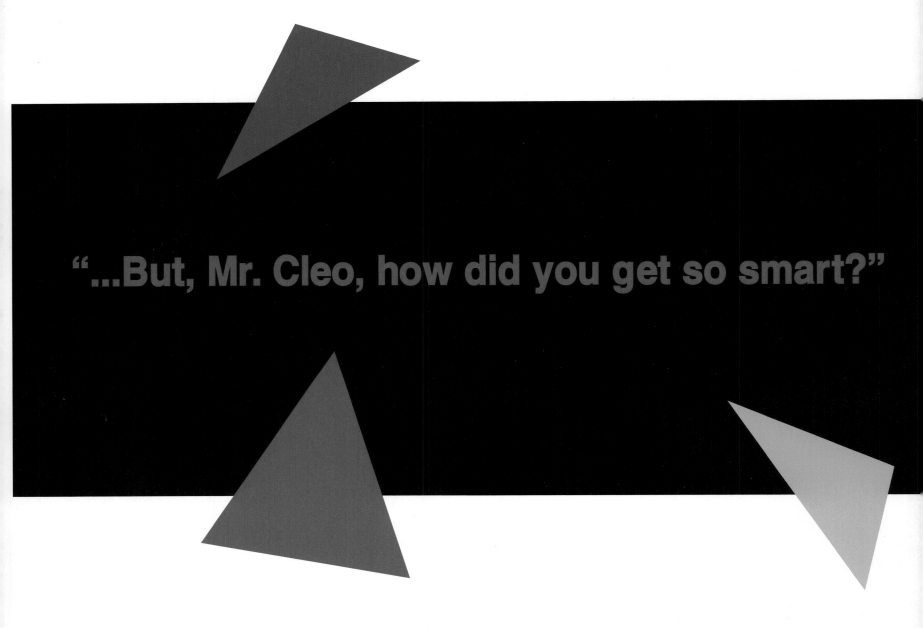

"...But, Mr. Cleo, how did you get so smart?"

Mr. Cleo

"**L**il' fellow, I never got through the 7th grade, cause I had to quit school to work on the farm with my daddy to help support my mom and younger sisters and brothers. But, I've been working at this school for 38 years now. I've spent many hours reading books in the library after mopping up, but most of the things I know, I had to learn the hard way.

"Remember, I had six children to grow up and go to college. They all helped me along with my education. Why, I got my GED when I was 52 years old. You're never too old to learn, Jamaal.

"Heck, I've taken a likin' to computers. Maybe I'll get one before I'm 80. You think?" said Mr. Cleo with a big smile on his face. "You can never know too much, but you can easily not know enough.

"Yeah, at 71 Jamaal," he sighed, "I've come a mighty long ways."

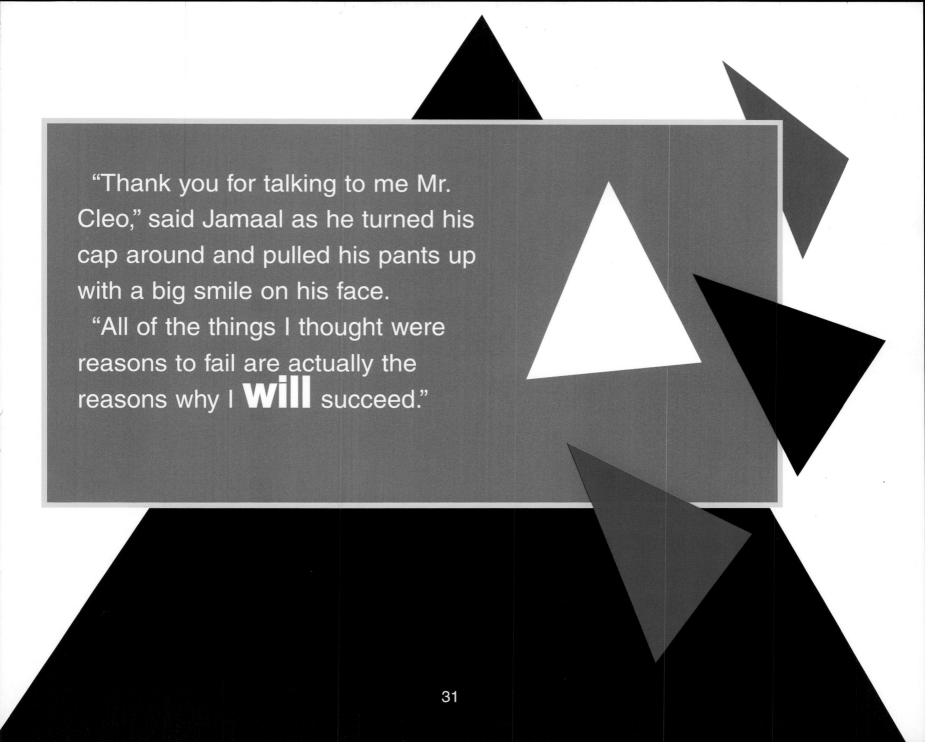

"Thank you for talking to me Mr. Cleo," said Jamaal as he turned his cap around and pulled his pants up with a big smile on his face.

"All of the things I thought were reasons to fail are actually the reasons why I **will** succeed."